Bridge to the Otherworld

Books by Cheryl Lafferty Eckl

Personal Growth & Transformation

A Beautiful Death:
Keeping the Promise of Love

A Beautiful Grief:
Reflections on Letting Go

The LIGHT Process:
Living on the Razor's Edge of Change

Wise Inner Counselor Books
Reflections on Being Your True Self in Any Situation
Reflections on Doing Your Great Work in Any Occupation
Reflections on Ineffable Love: from loss through grief to joy

Poetry for Inspiration & Beauty

Poetics of Soul & Fire

Bridge to the Otherworld

Idylls from the Garden of Spiritual Delights & Healing

Sparks of Celtic Mystery:
soul poems from Éire

A Beautiful Joy: Reunion with the Beloved
Through Transfiguring Love

Twin Flames Romance Novels

The Weaving:
A Novel of Twin Flames Through Time

Twin Flames of Éire Trilogy
The Ancients and The Call
The Water and The Flame
The Mystics and The Mystery

Bridge to the Otherworld

Cheryl Lafferty Eckl

FLYING CRANE PRESS

BRIDGE TO THE OTHERWORLD
© 2016, 2021, 2022 by Cheryl J. Eckl, LLC

Published by Flying Crane Press, Livingston, Montana 59047
Cheryl@CherylEckl.com | www.CherylEckl.com

All rights reserved. No part of this book may be used, reproduced, translated, electronically stored, or transmitted in any manner whatsoever without prior written permission from the author or publisher, except by reviewers, who may quote brief text-only passages in their reviews.

Library of Congress Control Number: 2015918793
ISBN: 978-0-9970376-0-9 (paperback)
ISBN: 978-0-9970376-1-6 (e-book)

Printed in the United States of America

*For courageous hearts
willing to cross the bridge
toward Home.*

Out of the Light
that beckons from the Otherworld
a thousand mystic voices sing:

*Embrace Love's deepest mystery,
the heart's way is the bridge.*

Opening the Way of Love's Mystery

Mystics gather
forces align
a veil parts
and stillness descends
in order that one may hear
truths not spoken aloud.

Here is the way of Love's mystery—

When its portal swings wide
the Heart opens to a thin place
where insight bestows its wisdom
like welcome rain upon a thirsty landscape.

Mind alone cannot cross this threshold;
soul conversation creates a bridge
to other worlds and wonders.

Contents

Opening the Way of Love's Mystery ix

Mystics Gather

    The Invitation 3
    Man of Wonders 5
    Brigid o' the Otherworld 8
    Taliesin 10
    Sisters of the Ruby Mantle 12
    Transfixed by the Compassionate Mother 13
    The Archangel 14
    Acceptance at the Top of the World 16
    The Master in Florence 18

Stillness Descends

    In the Glen at Sunrise 23
    Sean-nós 24
    Here Now 25
    Untold Treasure 26
    The Gift 27
    The Visitor 28
    Solitude and Simplicity 30
    The Still Point 32

The Portal Swings Wide

    Anticipating Adventure 37
    Spiral Dancing 38
    A Poet's Desire 40
    Becoming 41

Unbecoming 42
New Moon 46
The Arrow. 47
Dancing on the Bridge. 48

The Heart Opens to a Thin Place

Love's Mystery. 53
The Gate That Opens 54
Perceval Awakens. 55
The Full Heart Is Strong in Its Convictions . . . 56
Epiphany 57
Love's Prophecy 58
Sweet Communion 60
Love's Essence 62
A Special Kind of Joy 64
Loving Who Is Here 65

Insight Bestows Its Wisdom

The Pull. 69
Samhain. 70
Soul Retrieval 73
Assembly in the Halls of Light 74
Pisces to Aquarius 76
Soul Geometry. 78
The Teacher 80
Conversation with the Muse. 82

Welcome Rain on a Thirsty Landscape

Rainbow Light 87
New Wings 88
Resilience 90
The Church Mouse 91
Light and Roses 92
Choosing 95
My Own Retreat 96
Oasis 97

Soul Conversation Creates a Bridge

Waking Up to Joy 101
Mind the Thresholds 102
Taking a Chance on the Bridge 104
Meeting My Soul on the Landing 106
Ending an Exile 108
Song of the Homeland 110
Touch of the Otherworld 112

Notes 117

ILLUSTRATIONS

Dreaming, aka October, Maxfield Parrish, 1928 viii

Fairies Looking Through a Gothic Arch, ... xiv
John Anster Fitzgerald, 1864

Forest Sunrise, Albert Bierstadt, 1830-1902 20

Psyche Entering Cupid's Garden, ... 34
John William Waterhouse, 1904

Ecstasy, Maxfield Parrish, 1929 50

Night Is Fled, Maxfield Parrish, 1918 66

Rainbow Over Paradise, Ross Brunson, 2015 84

Poet's Dream, Maxfield Parrish, 1901 98

*Light will lead to Light
if you follow all the way
to greet the Masters
in their home.*

The Invitation

Won't you come with me?

Let us be pilgrims together
along the path that leads
from what we see
to where
we only dare imagine.

Supernal realms await us
just beyond this sylvan glen,
and my heart longs
for us to share
a vision's celestial magic

where spirals of ethereal light
will take us deep
into illumined passages
glistening
with morning dew
and fairy stars
a-twinkle overhead.

Mystic sojourners are we
brought together
for a purpose
as heart to heart
and hand in hand
we go exploring

across the bridge
that Love has built
out of itself

to teach travelers like us
that other worlds
are joined by a numinous power

that none can wrest
away from hearts
attached as friends
forever loyal
in mutual devotion.

Please, take my hand,
let us embark.

Love's mystery is calling.

Man of Wonders

Out of misty Avalon he comes
trailing clouds of stardust

his purple robes streaming
in the winds of change

that swirl within and 'round
his sphere of power.

Worlds turn at his command,
seas rise and fall

while apple orchards blossom
in grateful recognition

of the sweetness in his gaze,
the twinkle in his eyes

and the delicate touch he lends
to Nature's frailest creatures.

Master of diplomacy is he
who moves among the high and mighty

urging peace and consolation
for the many not yet free.

He cares not for the treasures
they would shower upon him

knowing as he does
precipitation's alchemy

yet richly does he fashion
his habiliments
to seem as one of those
he would advise.

The game's afoot!
he likes to say

when dealing with the foxes
bent on raiding a nation's hen house

and chuckles when they find
the chicks have flown the coop

his prophet's eye foreseeing their plots
in time to rescue a meek
and unsuspecting flock.

But skirmishes
do not a strategy create,
and so he oft retires
into his secret cave

to ponder brighter futures
for the man- and woman-kind
he lives to serve

deciding at long last
to try again to reach them

with his Bardic arts
of story, song, and poetry

so that dampened hearts
might catch fire once more
and throw off their oppressors

through the sheer unconditioned joy
of knowing who they are in Truth.

Brigid o' the Otherworld

She came to Ireland
    bringing rainbow light
    angel song, eternal fire
    and blessings that flowed
    forth in gentle mercy
    from her outstretched hands.

The people loved her
    with their whole hearts
    and bade her stay
    with them forever
    as mother, guide
    and inspiration.

And so she merged
    into the land itself,
    infusing all that
    lived there upon
    with the essence
    of her Spirit

Reminding them
    to embrace the circle
    she gave them
    as emblem of
    her sure return
    in the seasons'
    faithful turnings.

They learned to
> hear her voice
> in laughing brooks
> and mighty rivers
> that dance
> across her landscape

Cherishing as sacred
> wells and waters
> that sprang up from
> her earthen bosom
> to bless and nourish
> all that thirst.

And in the twilight
> of the dawn and dusk
> they follow her still
> in prayerful peace
> back and forth
> in pure communion

Across the bridge
> to the Otherworld,
> forever kissed
> by moonbeams
> and her knowing smile.

Taliesin

A figure appears in twilight's glow
to answer our hearts' longing
for comfort and recovery
of the lost traditions
we once knew—
or are they truly gone for good?

Stepping into Dreamtime
at his gestured call
we discover them unspoiled by time—
heavenly powers and earthly guides
that carry us to seers' realms
where such ones as he abide.

Taliesin is his name—
beloved bard to ancient kings,
inspired master of poetry
who lives in deep communion
with all living things
and often shifts into their shapes
to expand his knowledge and his care
for all beings in his purview.

He takes his place with staff upraised
and parts the veil to other worlds
blessing us with lightning force
and honeyed eloquence of speech.

O soul, give ear as his song rings out
that we might be enlightened.

~

I am the salmon wise and sleek
I am the stream in which it swims

I am the song of Lammastide
I am the verse writ by the wind

I am the Spirit of the bards
I am the tales they long to tell

I am the secrets still untold
I am the mystery you know
Secure within your deepest soul

I am the one of shining brow
The poet renowned in ancient lore

I gather here in mystics' glen
To bid you seek me all the more

For I will lead you to the source
That is your home and also mine
To slip behind the screen of time
And find your Self inside a poem.

Sisters of the Ruby Mantle

Planets align in our favorite image—
A hologram of mystery's purpose
The calling of our ancient Selfhood
Closely shared, yet individual,
A promise made in ages past
And many times repeated since then
Yearning to be seen and fulfilled
Yet not ready until just now.

A cosmic birth-day, to be sure
Inspired by joy and admiration
And a lineage held in common,
Sent with power through the ethers
To out-picture in this lifetime
As companions on this journey.

Our souls agreed to help each other
And so we have for centuries
In preparation for awakening
That we might see the path before us
In its deeper sense, and import
Of our pledge to the ruby mantle
To bear our calling with soul and fire
In four-square love of our great sponsors.

How good it is to have sisters.

Transfixed by the Compassionate Mother

I could sit here for hours.
Me—the one who didn't meditate.

In her Presence, time is not
And I am gently slipping into
A welcome space of *I don't know.*

She watches with such cosmic calm—
The universe stands still
To receive her blessing
Or moves according to her gaze
Bestowing perfect joy on every star.

Life has changed since she arrived.
This room is now a holy place
Perhaps no longer on Earth's plane.

I'm like a fish
Caught in the net of her love
Begging never to be released.

The Archangel

It wasn't what I expected—
        visiting an archangel
        in his home by the turquoise water.

Soft enormity was the feeling,
        as if the entire valley
        were enfolded in his great wings.

This protection was neither
        armored nor vehement—
        though I've heard
        he can summon both.

It was simply there as a shield—
        impenetrable, flexible, effervescent
        made of faith and loving kindness.

Though depicted for centuries
        as sword-wielding, a dragon-slayer,
        Michael the Archangel
        does not fight as humans do.

Instead, he radiates magnificence—
        his brilliance pulsating
        day and night
        anywhere in cosmos.

His legions ride the solar wind
    like dancing aurora borealis—
    blazing curtains of security
    around all beings—weak or strong

For Michael's power knows no bounds
    surrounding worlds with his Love—
    blue lightning flares the natural retort
    to those who would attack his universe.

And while apocalyptic foes wage noisy war
    against the innocents of Earth,
    hurling thunderbolts and cannon fire

Angelic hosts follow Michael's lead,
    linking wings in a fiery shield
    that returns evil's outrageous barbs
    back upon those who launch them

In brilliant showers of sparks and flame—
    a fireworks display as seldom seen
    created by the Archangel's Light
    that simply swallows up the dark.

Acceptance at the Top of the World

Come unto me,
I heard the Great One call.

So up and up I went
As high as man's machines
Could take me,
Then further on foot
Until I reached the apex
Where his secret doorway
Shown out in the distance.

Ten thousand feet and more
He bade me climb
To stand against the gale
And gaze upon his fortress
Till my heart would burst
With love and longing

For I knew not what—
Except to learn
What he would teach me
If I could but scale
The greater summit
Of his dwelling place.

Only hearts on fire
Can reach such heights.

Mine felt as a weak flicker
Along side the majesty
Of his radiance

The One I've known so well
In ages past, and yet the One
I seem to falter before—
Even when he beckons.

There is a threshold
To his chamber.
For reasons still unclear
I have hesitated for fear
Of what he would ask.

Am I ready to surrender all,
To fulfill my sacred destiny
As the Alchemist's beloved—
His true and tested daughter?

Come unto me, he says again,
His voice aflame
With magnanimous Love.

I raise up tall, encouraged.
And this time I step forward
Into the warm embrace
Of his eternal acceptance.

The Master in Florence

Remember me from bygone days
As we walked over sloping hills
Amber, red, and verdant green
In the bright, warm Tuscan sun.

We wandered along old cobbled streets
Where narrow alleys beckoned us
To venture into ateliers
Of painters, sculptors, and musicians—
Creators of inspired works
Designed to lift the souls of those
Who longed to step into a dream
Of oneness with Love's mystery
That slumbered in their drowsy hearts.

Beauty was our calling then,
Perhaps more now than ages past;
That we might enliven burdened minds
To seek imagination's realm
To slip the chains of earthly woes
And sail amongst poetic stars—
Their own true habitation.

And so today's fresh intimacy
Goes deep to touch the wounds most raw
Revealing hurts, resistant doors
Long closed to Beauty's finest art.

Those portals need not stay locked tight;
My Presence holds their secret key
And bids you welcome ardor's flame
Though it turn your safe world upside down.

Remember me with every kiss
Devotion's honey-eyed expression
And trust my care that brought you here
To fulfill our ancient promises.

Though *destiny* may feel too large,
Its mythic path can lead you home
To the golden rooms you once knew well
Where you may likely yet create
The greatest opus of your life.

The veil now parts that you might see:
I wait in patience beside the bridge
Where bliss and action are conjoined—
The arc your sweet affection builds
A filigree of purest white
That sparkles like new-fallen snow.

Won't you step across, my dear,
And feel Love's balm, like fairy wings
That raise you up into my heart.

Come rest awhile, for Beauty's sake.

Stillness Descends

*Is it possible to be so open
as to hear the silent song
of Presence?*

In the Glen at Sunrise

Morning glides in on misty feet
as all of Nature opens sleepy eyes
in glad appreciation for dawn's first rays
that bathe the waking world
in golden luminescence.

Walk softly with me now
and you will see how land and sky
are wed in radiant communion
as gentle creatures bestir themselves
to greet the day full-heartedly
in unconditional happiness
that another morn is dawning.

One feels as if the Earth stands still
or holds its breath in silent awe—
a moment more before the sun
breaks over the horizon.

And as we watch, a solitary doe
arises from her nighttime nest
turns her head toward the East
stands perfectly in silhouette
then fades into the forest
as her kind have done with each sunrise
ten thousand years before today—
at peace upon the landscape.

Sean-nós

Be silent, still
until you feel the breath take you—
filling, emptying
moving the reed to tune
touching a secret place
that only the full heart knows.

The flame sparks
bursting with a bonfire's light
that contains all
expresses all
consumes all
and will not be denied.

Embrace that fire
in sound and step.

Become the song, the singer
and the breath.

Dance forth in jubilant exultation
knowing that you burn
with true Love's intensity.

And let yourself be lifted
on wings of inspiration
that hush the mind
with Spirit's spontaneous tones.

Here Now

Welcome silence
    dear one,
    lie down
    and be still.

Hearken
    to what
    you do not hear.

Feel the absence
    and be comfortable
    in emptiness.

Throwing rocks
    in still water
    is not the answer.

That comes only
    from the
    right question.

What does it take
    to live as
    the best of yourself?

Action alone
    will not
    tell you, Beloved.

Untold Treasure

Searching for true being
Beyond work, play, thoughts—
No making, producing, creating
Not even loving
As an activity of extension.

Being abides, occupies, dwells
Like a hovering spirit
Seated in suspended lotus
Radiating pure suchness
In breathless perfection.

This is the treasure
Neither sought nor found
That only travelers come upon
When they return at last to Home.

The Gift

My gift to you is my absence.
An odd delight—
Setting your heart to aching
Just when you felt it start to sing.

I did it for the Muse, you see.
She said you were too full
Of thoughts and deeds
That left her out of bounds;
Too occupied with your
Own desires to let hers in.

It would appear she's jealous—
Though better framed
As focused on the task at hand
And more mindful of cosmic timelines
Than some humans care to be.

Don't fret about the lovers;
They will take care of themselves.
The Muse needs only your full regard.
Her gifts require attention
And a clean, clear room
To hold her inspiration.

Enjoy your solitude;
For with the Muse
There really is no such thing as alone.

The Visitor

Make room for me, I beg you.
Your house is so full
I cannot even find a chair.

Won't you make me some tea
Clear a space for two
And come sit with me a while?

You've been calling, so I have come.
My calendar was clear this morning
But you could barely crack the door.

The shock on your face said it all:
You did not believe I would answer,
Though Grace always
Accepts her invitations.

Saddest of all
Is your regret and shame
For not having cleaned house.

Don't you know—
I am the merriest of maids?

Could you have opened the door
With a welcoming heart,
My Presence would have
Set all in order.

Yes, care of the physical is essential,
Knowing that you cannot perfect it;
That is my job.

Yours is to make tea
Clear the morning's debris
Send Light into the basement
And love me with the fullness
Of which you are able today.

The sun, the moon, and stars
Abide eternally in my peace.
These are the house-warming gifts
I offer from the folds of my garment.

Be with me as I am
In the stillness of this moment
And so you shall be also.

The kettle is boiling, my love.

Solitude and Simplicity

The day is mine to fashion.
A delicious possibility—
no obligations
except to
this sublime interval.

The moment is all that is;
and finding that *All*
is the work of a lifetime.

Today, however,
I will not plan
nor hope, nor wish
nor project.

The day is perfect as it is
and simple in its plainness.

That's the way with Presence;
it's uncluttered, clear
transparent in all the best ways

and able to fill or empty
as the highest need arises.

There is no rush, says Life,
take your time today.

Sit here
and learn to feel
the rhythm
of a universal heartbeat.

It is appropriate
to rest
in the valley
between peaks.

Not all work
involves locomotion,
as lakes and trees
will tell you

and some journeys
are best made
without taking
any steps at all.

Consider
soaking in silence
relaxing into
not this, not this.

Breathe into nothing
and experience pure being
as a verb.

The Still Point

Deep in Midwinter's heart
    a stillness waits
    to bless the rays of light
    that glisten
    through the darkness,
    not so much as to dispel
    but as to greet
    in equal verity;
    for consorts are they
    Night and Day—
    separated by the world's opinion
    though not their own.

Indeed, they dance
    nine thousand hours
    in a year;
    and none more grandly
    than today
    when Night puts off
    her ebony cloak,
    relinquishing
    her moonlit reign
    unto her mate, the Day
    who bows to her
    interior light
    as he ascends the throne
    that will be his
    till summer turns.

For Dark and Light
    both know
    their place
    and graciously
    step back
    in the fullness
    of their power
    to honor the other
    who seamlessly
    flows in—
    a natural exchange.

With silent care
    Night nurtures Day
    until his power
    warms and grows;
    and Day loves Night
    for her sage advice
    that earthly ears
    so seldom hear.

In the still point
    of Winter Solstice
    they know
    each other's worth
    and do their part
    to see the other
    blessedly fulfilled.

The Portal Swings Wide

*To embark upon the inner journey
is to open a door
frequented by dreamers.*

Anticipating Adventure

Expect the unexpected
but do not
watch for it.

It's shy
and does not wish
to be seen
until you have forgotten
to look.

Transformation will come
when you
give up trying.

Power may be given
but only
from the inside out.

Meaning shifts
and shapes
around your changes
and peace tiptoes in
by hindsight.

The inner journey
is a disappearing act
practiced by travelers
fond of losing their way.

Spiral Dancing

How do you move
    through
    your world?

What is the rhythm
    of your step
    or the form
    of the ripples
    you cause
    on water
    when you pass?

Spiral dancing
    flows two ways—

Into the center
    where opposites
    resolve
    and unity
    is all

Then out again
    carrying wise words
    and Phoenix Fire
    to heal
    the broken circle
    of your dreams.

If you would dance—

Learn to cultivate longing
    for the razor's edge
    where Light meets dark
    where known meets Unknown
    where creativity flourishes
    and the heart comes alive
    with possibility.

A Poet's Desire

The point is to soften
so a poem can slip in—
to open the heart's door
for Mystery's inspiration.

Poems are shy little things
even when grand or epic,
and rough thoughts or sounds
frighten them away.

Like rabbits, they get twitchy
and scamper off to hide,
never to return the same
because they have forgotten
who sent them
or what they meant to say.

Poems feel like letters
from the gods
and taste like ambrosia
on the tongue that speaks them.

To be worthy of such a gift
is a poet's true desire.

Becoming

Life is lived forward
with eyes full front
and sunrise on the horizon.

An occasional glance
in the rearview mirror
is useful

Though travelers who keep
their eyes on the road
go further than those
who stop to discuss the miles
they've already driven.

Time flows through the hourglass
and rivers run to the sea.

Flowers grow from the ground up
never quite repeating themselves
from one year to the next.

The wise branch out like shady oaks
and strengthen themselves
by reaching for the sun.

New thoughts are in order
and will emerge from novel adventures
that open unforeseen doors.

Unbecoming

An actor's life is made
    of many roles,
    costumes, masks
    false fronts and
    cloaks put on
    to play in the dark

    the footlights casting
    odd shadows
    distorting the image
    an audience sees

    even tricking
    the entertainer
    to believe in
    her own disguises.

The show goes on
    until the Master Director
    reveals a larger scene,
    offering an end
    to the illusion.

On that fair day
    the actor
    doffs her hat,
    puts off her coat
    of fabricated colors

washes her face and hands
and steps
into the daylight
of her greatest role.

To be one's truer Self
evokes a finer script—
one written
in the ethers

whose lines
can never be
rehearsed,
except by hearts
made pure
in the forgetting
of past dramas.

As the lights come up
on a brand new day,
this novel stage
is illumined
by a brighter radiance,
whose source
is hard to fix
in space,
reflected as it is
on polished floors

left gleaming
by a cleaning crew
who whisked away
the dusty props
that had become
distractions from
a truer inspiration.

Bidding *adieu*
    to worn-out
    characters
    is what
    calls her back
    to life these days

    unraveling coils
    of expectation—
    the trappings
    of other people's
    dreams and goals,
    assumed to be her own
    until Life should say
    otherwise

    while seeing that
    her useful skills,
    hard won in labor
    and in joy

are not rejected
nor forgot

though softer now
in practice,
more delicate
in beauty

as her native artistry
elicits
deeper
mysteries
that also raise
bystanders up
in courage borne
of heart's delight

so they might
likewise
step into
their own
sweet
unbecoming.

New Moon

glad tidings of new starts
happy friends and open doors

life is greening
amid the space
that intuition is requesting

once upon a time
he was uncertain
but cosmic properties
now prevail
when he allows them

rain and snow and soil
help plantings prosper

complicating life
has gone the way
of yesteryear

today invites abundant
smiling faces

The Arrow

Straight and true
>the arrow flies
>when it hits its mark.

The Master Fletcher
>chooses the finest feathers,
>silken fibers to cut
>the wind and shape the arc.

Wood and metal carry the intent
>and bear the tension
>of the archer's string

As she pulls back and back
>with perfect aim,
>to hold the focus
>of Spirit's eye
>until the heart says, *Now!*

And so am I released.

Dancing on the Bridge

There is a place where essence lives
    where clarity resides in peace
    and the blur of this world
    is brought sublimely into focus.

Those following the Celtic way
    still title it the Otherworld,
    which moderns call abnormal,
    though this side of the boundary
    is the place of most disturbance.

In moments of deep communion
    I find my way across the span—
    this mystic bridge I dance upon
    to reach beyond the veil.

I rarely stay there very long—
    more often just an instant
    to glean an answer or insight
    and then dart back
    to speak or write
    the words I've heard,
    or to describe
    the Love and Light
    I've carried home
    to the earthiness
    of Earth.

Prayer and practice
    smooth my steps
    and open up the portals
    of my mind and heart

For then inspiration
    may step upon
    Love's crystalline bridge

Where we join in a sacred dance
    that floods me
    with sensations
    of sight and sound
    combined

A full-bodied experience
    of instant joy
    prompting words
    that speak
    on behalf of
    Mystery.

The Heart Opens to a Thin Place

*Open wide your heart
to expressions of the Radiance
that shines forever
where Love is.*

Love's Mystery

I stand before a gossamer veil—
a threshold to the Otherworld
and wait to be invited in
for none may push across the bridge
to whom or what may lie beyond.

Now gazing up at a luminous sky
my heart burns in ecstasy
as celestial visions flood my soul
with memories of Spirit's grace,
and I am overwhelmed with joy.

In that sweet instant I recall
the secret of Love's mystery—
this holy realm is not elsewhere;
it lives forever where I am.

And so the Heart of Love opens wide
welcoming me to step once more
into a sphere of soul and fire—
the thin place my heart has become.

The Gate That Opens

The gate that opens
first guards the heart
until it should awaken
roused by Love's
tender kiss of resurrection
that bids the rose
unfold her petals of devotion,
even though winter's snow
has bathed the sleeping earth
in silent white.

Red as ruby, rich as crimson
a velvet pathway leads
to the heart's secret center—
a place of perfect balance
kept alight with passion of pure fire
that fuels Love's finest consummation
even as it burns out
all unlike itself
so that Love may go on loving
creating joy and grateful tears
as the heart aches
and then expands
to contain more of itself.

Perceval Awakens

When first I visited the mysterious castle
A numinous spectacle astounded my eyes
As ethereal beings walked in procession
Bearing artifacts of silver and gold
Before a Grail radiating pure Light.

And as the Vessel moved down the hall
Each guest received the precise food
That he or she desired most—
All by the power of the *Sangreal*
As it flowed about its service of Love.

But I did not ask what all this meant
And in my neglect the castle vanished
Until in my wandering I could hear
A Presence speak to me as in a dream—

> Your hero's journey leads through the heart
> Where Love is both the source and goal
> And your willingness to confront the dark
> Bequeaths strong mastery to serve.
>
> Only Spirit knows how to fill
> Each one's chalice with their own elixir
> Without losing a drop of holy water
> Or blistering a hand in constant pouring.
> Sacred cups are by Love's mystery fulfilled.

And so I awake to my soul's true quest—
My task is to become that Love.

The Full Heart Is Strong in Its Convictions
by Stephen Eckl

Every hour I wait
For your Love.
Now am I to wait no longer?

Do not disappoint;
We are very close.

My manhood—
Your divine nature.

Listen carefully.
Stay awhile.
I have time to burn.

Oh, consume me.
I am yours—
At last.

You've been here
So long.
Why would I bid you good-bye?

Epiphany
by Stephen Eckl

As this cold winter day
turns in the afternoon sun,
my house creaks.

The sudden sound of snow falling
from the trees above
momentarily dissipates the tension.

Oh, the joy from falling snow,
from the faith that the end is nearing,
that the future is full of life.

And that soon I will again feel
the fullness of your Fire.

Love's Prophecy

She had not met him
yet in life,
though she knew that time
would come when cycles turned.

And she would give
herself to him
as she had done
with but one other.

And when they felt
compelled to wed—
as, of course,
she sensed they would,
she also knew
what they would say
in mutual devotion:

I will go to sea with you, my love,
and sail with you
amongst the stars.
I'll ford with you
the streams of life
and walk the pathway
that we share
till time runs out
and our pilgrim staffs
retire unto the attic.

My love will never waver
and we shall stay
as fresh as sailors
on uncharted oceans

adventurers together
led only by
our hearts and souls
and never by convention
that would trap us
in security

in the niceties
of culture
that clips the wings
of meeker birds
who fear to soar
where dreamers go
and Spirit is truly Home.

Sweet Communion

Unseen and seen are here
forever wed
in conjugal bliss
in oneness
everlasting
and supreme.

Most human minds
believe the split
but those once 'wakened
never tire
in sharing miracles
of sweet communion

the special blend
of here and there
that transcends time
on a rainbow bridge.

Though gossamer thin
there is a veil
not meant to block
only to remind Earth's travelers
that they have entered
holy realms.

For viewed from Spirit's
vantage seat
the way stays open
for willing hearts
who love much
what they do not see

and cherish those
whose whispered touch
they know as real.

Love's Essence

Love longs for intimacy...

breath to breath
heart to heart

in deep embrace
of self and other
as the mystery
of one, not two

touching, kissing
in purest harmony

relaxing into the fluid *now*
that flows between
and all around affection

being present for one another

looking, gazing, seeing
noticing each other's gifts

remembering what came before
in kindness.

Opening to *come what may*
souls touch
and go deep
into ecstasy

as separation disappears
and dreams are born
of bliss
and consolation.

When hearts unite
opposites dissolve

and beloveds fall
into each other

never to return
as quite the same

having drunk
the essence
of Love's desire
for intimacy.

A Special Kind of Joy

One would hardly call it joy—
    this solid feeling in the heart
    that does not come from happiness
    but rather from the realization
    that one has forgotten to be sad
    on days of former tears
    brought on by memories
    of who and what
    no longer gladden one's life.

It would have been a silver day
    two decades and a half
    that instead slipped by unnoticed
    which made it
    all the more precious to feel
    one need not summon
    to recollection
    an essence that abides full-flowered
    in the deepest recesses of one's heart.

This joy is like a ruby rose
    that blooms forever in the center
    behind a hidden door
    what swings wide open
    at the first sign of gratitude
    to fill one's whole house
    with the fragrance
    of candlelight and clover.

Loving Who Is Here

I am with you forever
Where I have always been
Seated in the lotus
Of soul space
Awake to what's happening
Loving you in that music.

Many things have changed
As life has made its rounds
But my Presence in you
Has never wavered
Even when you forgot
To look for me anew.

Each day is fresh with
Love's possibility.
Remember to notice
How I am showing up
And you will see me shining through.

Blue skies or grey—it matters not.
I am the One who is here for Love
Always.

Insight Bestows Its Wisdom

*There is a song the soul sings
when it feels the sun of clear reality
shining on its face
and lighting its way Home.*

The Pull

What is this force?

This energy
that keeps me going
when life is murky
and only the next step
glimmers—though barely?

It guides the blind
inspires the lame
encourages the downtrodden.

I have been all of these
and may be yet again.

Still, in the midst of chaos
or shining inspiration
it is there

A power within me
that matches its cosmic partner
to pull me forward in joy.

Yes—in joy!
The great, shocking realization
that source and result are the same.

And Spirit in me is pleased.

Samhain

The new year starts
with mist and wind
as fairy folk (the *Aos Sí*)
come dancing out of hillside
mounds
into twilight gardens

to gaze through
brightened windows
at the humans
holding court within
who forgot the veil is thin tonight

and not again
till springtime will they see
with such perception
into Spirit lands
of Love and Light.

The clocks roll back
in modern times
as if to beg
for one more hour
before the dark days settle in
and mystery o'ertakes the thoughts
of old and young
who now prefer
to wander in a neon world

that honors neither soul nor sprite
but looks for answers
in metallic realms
that harden hearts
to woodland views
and mask the Otherworld's
bright joy.

To light a bonfire
in the heart
is the task
of this festive ritual

for safety's sake to foster
deep soul communion
that opens insight
into double worlds

and guides the seeker
over dusky roads
that must be trod
through the Unknown

if one is to reach
a threshold
of long-sought
soul awakening.

For ancients
understood Samhain
as more than
revelry and fun
to keep the fairy folk at bay
lest tricksters spoil
the year's best fruits.

The wise ones
saw it as the start
of a pilgrim's trek
of seven weeks
twixt harvest time
and Solstice eve

a secret journey
revealed to few
each week an opportunity
a choice, a key
to stoke more fire
of inner Light
from base to crown
in sacred circles
to realize one's radiant Self
at Midwinter's celebration.

Soul Retrieval

There is a purpose to life
hidden deep in the mysteries
of ages past
yet uniquely visible
to those who care to see.

Seekers look for the Way, the Tao
the pathless path up a mountain
that appears
when one stops looking.

All is metaphor and dream.
Initiation is real.
Movement helps.
Motion in stillness.
Silence in action.

Paradox seems to bar the door
though only when you push too hard.

Bits of soul are scattered as sparks.
Gather them up and bring them Home;
that is the only task.

You will need a well-woven basket.

Assembly in the Halls of Light

In mountains and deserts
    of faraway places
    where only mystics can
    scale the cliffs of oracular dreams,
    Masters of deep wisdom
    gather in their homes of Light
    long hidden from humanity.

At every level of sea and sky
    they sense a shift,
    a troubling of the waters
    for which many souls are not prepared
    despite a century's intercession
    on behalf of mankind's freedom.

And so they meet in council—
    a convocation of ancient friendships
    borne of mutual service
    throughout lifetimes
    both human and divine.

Crystalline walls surround them
    in a great hall
    beneath the mountain
    a million facets reflecting
    rays of purest gold and white
    radiating within and around
    each one's shining Presence.

Their hearts blaze up with ruby fire
    as a mighty gong is struck
    and the sacred *aum* resounds
    to begin their consultation.

Great Masters do not debate as humans do—
    their thoughts aren't hid from one another;
    and so they focus all their will
    on a tone of perfect unity
    in faith that from combined intent
    solutions will be known to all.

At energy's crescendo, a golden scroll appears
    on which is writ in finest script
    profound words that will direct
    the liberation of an age;
    and as all attend, a voice recites
    the promise that each one will keep:

As friendship is our highest bond
    so shall we now extend the same
    unerring loyalty to souls who choose
    to be no longer tied to forms,
    that we might meet them face to face
    release them from their darkest nights
    free their hearts from fear and shame
    unlock the prisons of their own making
    and bring them safely Home at last.

Pisces to Aquarius

Two fishes swim oppositely
    carrying duality in their fins
    bringing mixed messages
    confusion, and delay.

Or so it would seem to those
    caught in nets
    of right or left
    black or white
    up or down.

The answer feels inscrutable
    until one swims
    with fishes
    who are not blind
    to one another.

Those who attach
to single directions
    will never see
    the other's view.

But savvy fishes
    of all stripes
    awakened
    in their passing
    catch each other's eye
    and recognize

        that up is often
        more like down
        right as left
        black as white—
        which means, of course
        that opposites are sometimes
        jointly true.

Lightly holding paradox gives way
        to the Water Bearer
        who focuses
        on the moment's need
        and pays no heed
        to the double-mindedness
        of near-sighted swimmers

        choosing rather
        to live in the flow
        of the compassionate
        fluid present.

Soul Geometry

Each soul
a crystal chalice is,
a snowflake form
transparent
in its being,
made perfect
in its purpose,
enlightened
by its loving.

In schools of Light
we study how
the choice is made
to be more wise
to hold more grace
that Love may shine
more clearly

Though we have not
earthly words
to use for rainbow rays
or stardust shapes
that sing and dance
in ethereal skies,
blazing messages
of transcendence.

Illumination
is the game
that sunbeams play
with souls who wait
for centuries or days
to plot their course anew
and walk upon the Earth
once more
to polish brighter facets
on their cups
of conscious living.

The Teacher

I bought his photo at a fair

> an arresting image
> captured by a photographer
> who had been gifted
> with a rare close-up
> of the face full on

> the penetrating golden eyes
> looking back through the lens
> with a startling intensity
> that carries no malice

> only a present awareness
> that seems to have witnessed
> the eternal flow of life
> and to have accepted
> his role in it.

Here is a teacher I can trust

> a clear thought arising
> as his gaze met mine
> in mutual recognition and respect
> for one another's place
> in the chain of being

> and perhaps my realization
> that his wisdom simply flows
> into open hearts
> because he does not care to teach.

He has no need of students

      nor of sycophants
      though there are many
      who worship his lineage
      as I myself have done
      and would be tempted
      once again

      were it not for
      his clear admonition
      that only those
      who embrace their essence
      can meet him in his

      as a pure white arctic wolf
      known to Native peoples
      as Teacher

      born of the Dog Star
      come to Earth
      to show us humans
      how to be here.

Conversation with the Muse

I find it amusing, she said with a wink
        that you think of me as masculine;
        my speaking to you with precision
        does not negate a feminine aspect.

Breathe now and feel into our connection.

Does not loving kindness
        accompany gentle compassion
        as my firm love bids you
        come up higher in consciousness
        while settling deeper
        into your True Selfhood?

Your thoughts of male and female
        would divide me
        where I am not separate.

Beauty, Truth, and Goodness
        call us into transcendence
        where we are not two, but one.

I am in you as you are in me—
        drinking in soul essence
        warmed by Spirit's fire
        resting in the body's ground
        that holds us safely
        in Love's confident arms of unity.

We only speak of parts
>   so we might offer clarity.

Your heart knows the truth:
>   I am the voice of inner knowing
>   the Wise Inner Counselor
>   the one who speaks on behalf of all
>
>   your most loyal friend
>   and riverbed for the inspiration
>   that links you with the Cosmos.

Please welcome me in my many guises;
I enjoy playing dress-up.

Welcome Rain on a Thirsty Landscape

*Inspiration is too big for words,
too faint—except to feel it coming
and to know one's Self
in its alignment.*

Rainbow Light

One need not die to step across
the bridge between worlds
though they who live
may struggle in the journey
back and forth.

If we only knew how thin the veil
when pure Love opens
hearts to hearts
we'd rush with joy to enter in
to sweet moments of communion

Which angels long to share with those
who suffer from a cold belief
in borders and stark boundaries
that simply are impossible
in the rainbow Light that joins us.

New Wings

The sky had always beckoned
    though earthlings
    don't have wings—
    or so he'd thought.

Grounded was how he'd felt
    except in his dreams—
    the ones he mostly
    didn't remember.

What if, he wondered
    regular wings
    weren't necessary at all
    but only a light heart
    that could soar
    to great heights

Not limited by time or space
    and truly free
    in Eternity's holy instant,
    buoyed by grace
    suspended in joy

And so full of Love
    that rays of Light
    would act like boosters
    to lift him out
    of his mundane life?

The realization flashed
    into his heart:

There was no ballast now
    no fear
    no reason
    not to commune
    with angels
    day or night

    and liberate
    his soul at last

    to fly straight Home
    to Spirit's realm
    in his simplest
    meditation.

Resilience

To believe the unbelievable
to see life from a cosmic view
to accept that
the unacceptable occurred

and then to bounce back
from desperation—
this is the path of liberation.

To be resilient is a grace
potentially bestowed on all,
especially the joyous
who will walk through fire
and brave the darkest storms

in order that others may live
to see a brighter day
to come through unscathed
as if nothing had ever happened
and no one had been injured.

The soul may be bruised
but is not scarred forever
when Love is realized
as its perpetual, eternal essence.

The Church Mouse

Some ideas are planted early—
Such as living at church.

Not just attending, but abiding
Midst candles, incense
And the resonance of organ pipes
Vibrating the tall stone arches
Wooden pews, and stained glass windows.

Imagine having the place to myself—
She finds the thought exhilarating

Of wandering up and down long aisles
Visiting with saints and angels
Kneeling anywhere she likes
Or venturing to the altar
To see if that man ever comes down
Off the cross to rest.

The pulpit offers her favorite view:
Looking out upon
Her invisible congregation

Hoping for a spiritual sign
And wondering if one so small
Could ever feel the touch of grace
That fills this place
When she is all alone at church.

Light and Roses

Two sisters part the veil
twixt here and there
between this side
and the other.

Grief is one
who is well known;
she has her own agenda
and follows her own will
for few would choose
to call her.

Though a miracle worker
she comes unbidden
in the wake
of dire circumstance.

Loss is the key she uses
to open the door to Truth
to the deeper Self
to possibilities
one would not seek

even as they light the path
to future happiness
on the roller coaster
that is Grief's way.

Joy has been known
to follow her sister, Grief
tidying up the frayed
thoughts and feelings
left in mourning's
dark passages.

Most think of her
as the kinder sister
the perky one
the easy-going sprite
whose path leads straight
to relaxation, happiness, and calm.

They bid her come
in myriad ways
then wonder at her absence
in the hollowness
of earthly distractions
remedies and toys.

For the secret
known to sages and to children
is that joy is the natural state
of those who entertain life
as a game played best
with a light touch
of which the ego is incapable.

Joy inhabits the receptive heart
made empty of conditions
that lock the door
to Spirit's deepest knowing.

We only lose what we do not need.

Stepping through the gap
with Grief as gracious hostess
clears the way for Sister Joy

who comes to stay
and bless life forever
with her fragrance
of Light and Roses.

Choosing

Tomorrow's poem
comes flowing through—
receive it into your heart.

It enters through
the gateless gate
the pathless path.

There is no tomorrow—
only this tender moment
when petals open
to receive the dawn and dew
of sweet Presence.

Such is the life when chosen.

Or when one is chosen
to live in the stream,
happily immersed in the tide
of being blessed.

My Own Retreat

Stay home—
>that's the message
>from body, mind, and Spirit.

Be at peace in your own skin
>in the depths of
>your own heart.

This is the true thin place—
>the connecting point
>for all you seek
>within and without.

No need to venture beyond these shores.

We have lakes aplenty
>still waters, and gentle streams
>to bring you Home
>to where you've longed
>for rest and recreation.

Everything you need is here.

Dive deep into this reality
>and swim in the lake
>of soul comfort and Truth.

Stay home and find your Self.

Oasis

Everyone needs a safe haven
  a secret place of respite
    from a chaotic world
  a heart space of peace
    and acceptance.

I am that place, Beloved.

Seek me in the folded pages
of your memories.

Listen for the rustle of my garments.

Feel my Love enfold you
in your darkest hour
and know me as the sanctuary
whose door is always open.

Soul Conversation Creates a Bridge

*Sometimes to move forward
you have to go back
and pick up what or whom
you forgot to love.*

Waking Up to Joy

It's not that hard
>if you put your mind to it—
>deciding to breathe in the morning.

Even welcoming aches and pains
>as the body's invitation
>to pay attention

>>to partner for the day
>>in mutual admiration
>>between body, mind, and Spirit

>>who do each other the best of service
>>when leaning in together.

Absence makes the heart grow fretful
>when body loses touch with mind
>and Spirit wanders back to heaven.

Reunion lies in sparking joy—
>the ignition and the engine
>that keeps the centers spinning

>>so every part of life is filled
>>with the joy of waking up today.

Mind the Thresholds

Life is precarious at transition points
    where the soul steps out
        once again into uncharted waters.

Flush with accomplishment
    she may be reckless—
    a bit too sure of future success
    even greedy for what comes next.

Mind the gap, as they say;
    fortunes can slip from our grasp
    in the split second
    between here and there.

For there is always an interval—
    the in-breath e're action is taken
    a moment of decision:
        What to do
        and how to be
        in the doing.

At the cliff edge—
    in the mist of expectation
    and the gathering storm
    of possibility
    nothing is clear.

Life begins anew each time
        a turning point is reached
        for past is always prologue
        and genius never guaranteed.

Mind the thresholds
        so your transformation
        may be complete
        the butterfly fully formed
        and the hands of your clock
        ticking happy hours
        for cycles without ending.

Many fear the razor's edge—
        the ineluctable choice
        to take what seems
        a perilous chance.

But saying *Yes!* to the Unknown
        can bring life's
        greatest blessings.

What will you say, my dear?

Taking a Chance on the Bridge

This is where you get out, he said.

Not the cozy village you'd expected—
    with shops and tidy streets
    park benches, tea rooms
    hanging baskets of bright flowers:
        familiar sights all scrubbed up
        for tourists.

For you, the end of the line comes
    at a narrow pull-off
    just past a crossroads
    you did not note as special.

With all your friends heading off
    to a mountain ramble
    your destination is a singular pub
    back over a bridge
    you did not know you'd crossed—
        the final span marking a fulfillment
        the point of no return and a choice.

Watch out for bachelor farmers, they called.
    If they start numbering their acres
    we may not see you again!

It happened once, the story goes,
    when a lady traveler
    ran away with a charmer
    she met in such a place.

But you're not looking for romance.

Your choice is simpler:
> to sit in a corner
> and write gloomy verse
>> or to speak out of your vulnerability
>> and ask for directions.

Sometimes that's all it takes
> to restart the engine of life—
> a word of inquiry that
> honors hospitality.

And suddenly you're talking
> with new friends
> sharing stories
> a pint or two
> and common observations.

Not realizing until later
> that the humblest of conversations
> has deposited in your heart
> a passport to hope
>> the end of life
>> as you've known it
>> and the way
>> to future joyous outcomes.

Meeting My Soul on the Landing

Nobody tells you about the secret staircase.

You must discover it yourself by accident
When on an idle day's explore
Following a vision you hope is true
Of hidden places that might exist
In your own deep heart of hearts.

It's a steep climb that twists and turns
As if going on forever
Or at least to the top of the Statue of Liberty
Though not like that ascent at all.

Neither dark nor cold nor metallic—
The higher you climb, the lighter, warmer
Cozier, and more colorfully home-like
Each step becomes
Radiating an iridescence
Whose shimmer masks the effort required
To mount progressive flights.

For this is not a single set of stairs—
More like gradations that have landings
Made for resting and for celebrating
What you achieved to reach this dimension

Where time is not what you thought
And there is no competition
To reach the top.

Today's ascent is different from
The ones I've made before.

And, yes, I recollect now many climbs
Though none so far or magical
Or vibrant with expectancy.

For as I sit, gazing up
At more bright steps
A Presence joins me on my bench
Looks into my eyes with purest Love

And greets me as my own True Self—
The soul of my belonging.

Ending an Exile

My soul is homesick.
I felt the longing yesterday
when it leapt up in my belly
while watching a film
about cathedrals, classical domes
and stained glass windows.

I love to sit in Gothic churches—
to revel in the glory
of radiantly colored sunbeams
streaming through
crystalline rose patterns
and translucent images
of saints and angels

to feel myself enfolded
in the devotion
of ancient hearts and hands
who toiled
to build these marvels
that reminded them
of their first and final Home.

Look up! the tall spires
seem to beckon
and bid your soul
keep up the climb.

Weary not, fair one,
even when the way feels dark
connection lost
and past accomplishments
a waste of time.

Your essence is a mighty thing—
more powerful
and filled with Love
than you could ever imagine.

Go be that Love
with heart and hand
and build your own cathedral
of true being.

This is how to end
your soul's long exile
here in earthly realms
while serving
all the beloved ones
you have for lifetimes
sought to save.

Song of the Homeland

Haunting—
as the soul-stirring tone
of Uilleann pipes
echoing across lakes and fells
calling me back
to a place of soft recollection
all mossy green and misty
in the twilight realm
twixt wakefulness and sleep.

A song not heard for eons
yet familiar as my heartbeat
close as breath itself
that sighs out
for lost companions
who come again in new apparel
to sit with me upon the hillside
conjuring memories
of what, we do not know.

Except we hear its melody—
the music of our passage Home
its lyrics writ in ancient words
that taste of joy
upon the tongue
that longs to speak them
once again.

And sing the song
that tunes the heart
to soulful travels
heroic journeys
that must be undertaken
before the misty piper
can play his final note.

Till then—
we hear but echoes
in the distance
reminding us to still the mind
in peaceful attention
that kindles soul fire
from the music of what's happening;
resounding in our bodies
growing louder as space narrows.

For Homeland's song
knows neither here nor there
has never stopped
and never will
even when we cease traveling.

We only long
for what we think is missing.

Touch of the Otherworld

I have
found you
in my heart

and I will
always be
in yours.

My love
knows
no bounds
no obstacles
nor barriers
no beginning
and no end.

As we
have been
so shall
we ever
be
in the
radiance
of this
finer place
that opens
when you say
I will.

Joy lives
beyond the veil
golden pink
and glowing
with unconditional
all-pervasive
all-enfolding
Love

indivisible
wonder
of flowers
fawns
and foliage
basking
in perfect
sunshine

and the unity
of knowing
all is right
in this
eternal moment
that wipes away
all tears
with its
effulgence
of pure being.

Once
touched
by Love's
immensity
your world
will never
be the same

forever
infused
with the scent
of earth
after
the rain,
the taste
of roses
and of violets

a thousand
brilliant hues
of rainbow ray

glistening
through
misty waterfalls
that bathe
the scene
in liquid Light.

We
are fluid
now

swimming
to and fro
across
a pool
of silky
warmth
under a
deep blue
canopy
of stars
that twinkle
a welcome
song

*This, too
will be
your
Home.*

*There is
no other
world
than
Here.*

Notes

Bridge to the Otherworld is inspired by the Celtic belief in a world parallel to our own that is peopled by a supernatural race of beings known as *Tuatha Dé Dannan*, as well as elementals, fairies (the *Aos Sí*), and spirits of the deceased who remain close to their loved ones, even after death.

Since claiming my Irish heritage as a Lafferty descendent, I have most profoundly felt the presence of the Otherworld and its etheral residents. They all have had a hand in creating these poems.

Here are a few explanatory notes:

Brigid o' the Otherworld: The Celtic goddess Brigid is considered the patroness of poetry, smithing, medicine, arts and crafts, cattle and other livestock, sacred wells, serpents (in Scotland) and the arrival of early spring.

Her festival day, *Imbolc* (celebrated February 1), is traditionally a time for weather prognostication.

See Wikipedia's excellent article for more detail.

The historical St. Brigid of Kildare was born at a time of major transition in 5th century Ireland, so she is said to embody both the pre-Christian Celtic and later Christian Celtic spirit. In fact, some scholars credit St. Brigid with pioneering monastic life in Ireland.

It is generally accepted that she built her double monastery for men and women in Kildare around 470 AD. Her monastery was acclaimed as a center of education, pilgrimage, worship, and hospitality until the 16th century when all the monasteries were suppressed. Source: https://solasbhride.ie/

For more information—https://www.brigidine.org.au. Accessed July 2022.

Taliesin: The historical Taliesin was a renowned bard who is believed to have sung at the courts of at least three Brythonic (ancient Briton/Celtic) kings in 6th century England.

He is also a mythical figure who has been associated with an ancient version of Merlin. This myth is documented in *The Search for Merlin* by Nikolai Tolstoy.

For a fictionalized account of Taliesin's life see *Radiant Brow: The Epic of Taliesin* by H. Catherine Watling.

Transfixed by the Compassionate Mother: This is my meditation on the exquisite oil painting titled *Universe of Compassion* by Marie Antoinette Kelley. Life changed when I brought it into my home. For more information about this inspired artist's work, see https://makfineart.com/ Accessed July 2022

The Archangel: This poem was written after a visit to Lake Louise near Banff in the Canadian Rocky Mountains. Archangel Michael is said to maintain an etheric retreat at this beautiful site.

Sean-nós: *Sean-nós* is a type of traditional Irish acapella singing noted for its ornamentation and improvisational style.

Perceval Awakens: The inspiration for this poem comes from a depiction of Perceval's quest in *The Grail Legend* by Emma Jung and Marie-Louise von Franz.

The Full Heart Is Strong in Its Convictions: Written by the late Stephen Eckl (1952-2008) on December 18, 2004.

Epiphany: Stephen Eckl, January 6, 2005.

Samhain: *Samhain* (pronounced "sow-en") is an ancient Celtic holiday that is celebrated beginning at sundown October 31 through November 1. To the Celts it is a time of harvest and signifies the beginning of a new year.

The Teacher: Wolf is a Native American power animal and spirit guide, known in many traditions as Teacher.

Taking a Chance on the Bridge: This is a true story that took place at a pub across the bridge at Maam (pronounced *mahm*) in Western Ireland, on the road from County Clare to Connemarra.

Song of the Homeland: Uillean pipes (pronounced "illen") are traditional Irish bagpipes that are played by squeezing a bellows under the arm, rather than blowing into them as with Scottish pipes.

Acknowledgements

I have heard it said that gratitude opens the way to all other blessings. Life has proved to me the truth of that statement many times over.

I know of several people who create gratitude journals as a practice that keeps them in that attitude—to maintain the open heart and mind that gratitude nurtures.

For me, writing poetry has the same effect of opening my heart and mind to a flow of enlightening experience.

The poetical atmosphere is a mystical space, a realm of consciousness to which I find myself homing. The opportunity to visit that place and live there for periods of time is a grace for which I am eternally grateful.

The muse is a marvelous aspect of being. I do not pretend to fully understand her or him. Inspiration appears in a number of guises. And isn't that part of the beautiful mystery that has for centuries beckoned poets to brave the Unknown in hopes of coming out the other side with a few lines that may delight or inspire or even heal.

Such is my experience and a profound reason for the gratitude I am offering here along with profound thanks to my colleagues Theresa McNicholas, James Bennett, and Paula Kehoe. Additional thanks to Ross Brunson for the gorgeous rainbow photo he let me use, and to the artists whose public domain images we have selected for this volume.

May you, dear reader, feel my gratitude flow from these verses. Writing them has been a gift that I am joyfully grateful to share.

A Poet of Soul & Fire

Cheryl Lafferty Eckl is a mystical poetess and storyteller who writes in the ecstatic tradition of Rumi and Hafiz.

She lives in Livingston, Montana, where she finds profound inspiration in the surrounding mountains, rivers, lakes, and Big Sky spaces that have long been recognized as places of spiritual connection and healing.

An award-winning author of multiple books, Cheryl continues to embrace life's myriad transitions as she writes, teaches, and pays deep attention to the poetics of her soul.

To learn more about her work, please visit her website at www.CherylEckl.com.

www.ingramcontent.com/pod-product-compliance
Lightning Source LLC
Chambersburg PA
CBHW021129300426
44113CB00006B/357